THE GHOST STORIES

Alan Toner

Copyright © 2016 Alan Toner
All rights reserved.
ISBN: 1523288035
ISBN-13: 978-1523288038

Acknowledgements

This book is dedicated to Harry Price, Britain's most famous ghost hunter.

Contents

1. Blackpool Ghosts..1
2. The Wirral Museum..3
3. Irish Ghosts..5
4. Haunted Chester...9
5. St. George's Hall...12
6. The South Shields Poltergeist...14
7. The Enfield Poltergeist..16
8. The Whaley House..19
9. Sexual Ghosts..22
10. The Amityville Horror...25
11. Harry Price..28
12. Ghosts of The Titanic..33
13. Haunted Shops and Stores...36
14. The Fleece Inn..43
15. Interactive Ghosts..45
16. The Ghosts of Charles Dickens...................................47
17. The Ghosts of Pluckley Village....................................50
18. The Winchester House...52
19. Ordsall Hall..55
20. The Ancient Ram Inn..57
21. Pengersick Castle..59
22. Tutbury Castle..61
23. Bodmin Jail..63
24. Woodchester Mansion...65
25. Derby Gaol 67
About The Author..70

1. Blackpool Ghosts

Blackpool is the UK's most popular seaside resort. For years, thousands of holidaymakers from all over the British Isles and the world have flocked to the Lancashire town to take in its many attractions, from its famous Golden Mile and its illuminations to its wonderful sandy beach.

But aside from its famous tourist attractions, Blackpool also has the odd resident ghost or two.

The most notable one that has been reported is the phantom that is said to haunt the Ghost Train at Blackpool Pleasure Beach. The ghost goes by the name of "Cloggy", so called because he is the spirit of a ride operator who used to wear clogs. Witnesses claimed to have heard Cloggy walking around inside the Ghost Train, the sound of his clogs clattering on the tracks making an eerie, spine-chilling sound. Many of the staff there have reported hearing these strange footsteps.

Cloggy died about 20 years ago, but his is not the only spirit that haunts Blackpool's attractions. His friends include a possible female ghost in the Arena. There are also spectres in the Star Pub and Sir Hiram Maxim's Gift Shop.

Staff working late at night, walking across to the tractor bay, have felt really cold, chilled to the bone and an "awful" presence. At the Star Pub there have been sightings of shadows and a male figure in the cellar, living accommodation and Morgan and Griffin Bars. He is said to bear a resemblance to Karl Marx. Five years ago, two workmen claim to have spotted him.

Four years ago, a figure was seen at 3am walking through the bar before disappearing.

The ghost of a small female child, aged about nine, is said to have been seen at Sir Hiram Maxim's Gift Shop. Sir Hiram Maxim's Flying Machines is the oldest ride at the park, built in 1904. And about three years ago, an item moved itself overnight to a completely different spot.

You might think that all these spooky happenings would frighten the punters off. On the contrary, they're still flocking to the Pleasure Beach where the ghosts are seen as part of its rich history.

2. The Wirral Museum

Situated in Hamilton Square, Birkenhead, the Wirral Museum - formerly the old Birkenhead Town Hall - has a number of ghosts which have been seen by members of staff and the general public over the years.

A figure of a man has often been sighted sitting on a bench close by the main entrance after the museum has been closed up for the night. This apparition sits quietly for a while, then suddenly disappears into thin air.

There is also the ghost of a young girl called Nellie Clarke, who was murdered near the Town Hall in 1925 after attending a New Year's party given by the mayor for war orphans.

The other reported ghost is that of a man who has been caught on CCTV walking along a locked-up corridor. Initially deeming him to be an intruder, the security guards immediately rushed to nab the man. But they were shocked to find that when they searched all the corridors and rooms in the building, the figure had mysteriously vanished.

Other strange occurrences that have been reported at the museum are the sounds of a party in full swing, piano playing coming from the ballroom, glasses clinking, Victorian style wallpaper being mysteriously pasted back up, and the sound of a woman's long dress swishing along the floor behind one of the members of staff.

As the town hall has held many lavish parties and grand

Alan Toner

events over the years, all these strange happenings could very well be the ghosts of long dead revellers.

3. Irish Ghosts

Ireland is a country that has its fair share of ghosts. As well as being the land most associated with fairies, leprechauns and banshees, the Emerald Isle has also seen many cases of spirit hauntings over the years. Moreover, these hauntings have not just been confined to old churchyards either, but have also been reported in towns, cities, police stations and railways sheds. In addition, dozens of haunted castles and houses pepper the land.

Leap Castle, an old fortress belonging to the O'Carrolls near Bear in County Offaly, is said to be one of the most haunted castles in Ireland. A man sleeping there reported feeling a strange coldness gripping his heart, even though the room was not cold at the time. Then, standing at the foot of the bed, he was stunned to see the tall figure of a woman, dressed in red attire. As he reached for his matchbox to strike a match, the figure mysteriously vanished into thin air.

Another strange incident was the experience of the lady of Leap Castle. Whilst in the gallery that runs above the great hall, she felt two hands placing themselves on her shoulders. Simultaneously, there was a horrible stench of decay, like that of a decomposing corpse. When she turned around, she saw that standing right behind her was a creature that resembled a human in form, though it couldn't have been more than four feet high. The strange entity had two black holes where its eyes should have been. As the woman gazed in utter horror at the nameless thing, it just disappeared, as did the foul stench that accompanied it.

Other paranormal occurrences that have been reported at Leap Castle are: the ghosts of a little old man and woman, dressed in old fashioned clothes; a cowled figure, resembling a monk, walking through the window of a room in the castle; and - often described as the "Head Ghost" of Leap Castle - the spirit of a priest, who was murdered in the castle's chapel (the so-called "Bloody Chapel") in 1532 by his own brother.

Ross House is a country residence just above Clew Bay, and there have been many reports of ghostly activity here. The spirit of a former maidservant has been sighted in the bedroom and on the stairs. Ghostly footsteps have been heard going up and down a staircase that is no longer there. Strange figures have been seen sitting before the fire in the drawing room, and at the window of the same room, a man once reported seeing a "terrible face."

Rahona Lodge, at Carrigaholt, County Clare, was the summer home of the Keane family. In 1917, Charlotte Keane wrote of the ghostly apparition in the "little dark room facing west." The house certainly did have a rather creepy atmosphere, as many locals would never venture near it at night.

A Phantom Train has been reported at a railway station, on the now closed-down line from Clones to Armagh. On a warm summer evening in 1924, two men were waiting for a train. It was quiet in the station, and there was nobody else there waiting but themselves. As they sat there on a platform bench, they suddenly heard the sound of voices coming from inside the waiting room. The voices were hushed, and accompanied by strange moans and groans. These weird sounds grew louder and louder, until finally one of the men got up and pressed his face against the waiting room window, to see what on earth was going on in there. He was shocked to see that the narrow room, containing just two benches and a long table, had nobody in there at all. Then, when he resumed his seat, the man heard the sound of an approaching train. Raising themselves to their feet, they looked down the line. The noise reached a peak, and they involuntarily jumped back as they heard a terrifying scream, right when the engine seemed to rush past them with a loud whistle. However, despite the sound, no train appeared. The sound faded away, the tracks still as empty as before. The two men sank back down on the bench, looking at each other in utter shock and disbelief.

When the signalman came out of his office a few moments later, he told them that he himself had heard nothing, but then related to them the story of a man who had jumped in front of a train at the station a year before. When the man was brought, seriously injured, into the waiting room, nothing could be done to save his life, he sadly died there on the long table.

Charleville Castle is regarded as the finest Gothic Revival building in Ireland. Charleville castle is bordering the town of Tullamore, near the Shannon River. The castle is situated in Ireland's most ancient primordial oak woods, once the haunting grounds of Ireland's druids.

The word 'druid' in Gaelic means, "knower of the oak". The castle is said to be haunted by the ghost of a young girl who fell down some stairs to her death in the early 1800s. The girl still roams around the castle, and can be heard in rooms above moving furniture around, laughing and talking. The castle has been the subject of many paranormal investigation groups from around the world.

Alan Toner

The Shelbourne Hotel, situated in Dublin, has its own resident ghost. Whilst staying at the hotel in August 1965, Hans Holzer, the American ghost hunter, was in Dublin conducting an investigation of hauntings in and around the city, and was very surprised to come across this ghost in the hotel. Sybil Leek, the British medium, who, together with Holzer's wife, was accompanying him on this investigation of Dublin's ghosts, experienced the ghost in her small top-floor room. Whilst lying awake in bed just after two o'clock in the morning, she heard a noise that sounded like a child crying. When she called out, "What is the matter?" she heard a small voice answer, "I'm frightened." Then, when Miss Leek invited her to come into her room, she felt a small figure climb onto her bed, and a light woolly material brush against her cheek and her right arm. When she awoke in the morning, her arm felt numb, like a weight had been pressing on it. The next evening, Miss Leek spoke to the ghost, that of a girl aged seven. The ghost said her name was Mary Masters.

The following night, Miss Leek went into a trance and held a conversation with Mary. However, Miss Leek could recall nothing of the conversation when she came to again. Hans Holzer noted that the child seemed to be ill, perhaps from a cold or bad throat, and was asking for a big sister named Sophie. Holzer then concluded that the ghost was that of a child who had died in one of the group of houses that the Shelbourne Hotel had been constructed from. The child had died around 1846, and this was the date that Sybil Leek had found herself writing down the day before.

4. Haunted Chester

Chester is one of Britain's most ancient cities, and is particularly noted for its many historical buildings and attractions, especially in regard to the Romans. Not surprisingly, with all this history, Chester has earned a reputation for being the UK's most haunted city.

Over the years, there have been many reports of all kinds of ghostly sightings and other paranormal phenomena. With its narrow streets and alleyways, not to mention its fascinating crypts and cellars - many of which are situated beneath popular shops, pubs and restaurants - Chester can certainly offer a compelling record of well-documented ghosts, hauntings, apparitions, spooks and poltergeists from almost every century across two thousand years.

Below are just some of the places in Chester that are said to harbour various ghosts and poltergeists:

1. Thornton's Chocolate Shop, Eastgate Street - Three ghosts are said to haunt this shop: a poltergeist known as "Sarah," who was jilted on her wedding day, and is the best-known spirit in Chester. She is said to move objects and shove people when they are on the stairs; the ghost of a large jovial-looking man dressed in an apron, who has been seen in various parts of the building; and finally, the third paranormal entity is described as an "insubstantial, almost invisible, male spirit."

2. W.H. Samuel's, Foregate Street - This jeweller's store is

reputed to be haunted by a ghost called "George." Staff working there have experienced many strange things, which they attribute to this entity.

3. Watergates Crypt, Watergate Street - The ghost of a long dead seaman is said to roam around this wine bar.

4. Watergate Row - The ghost of a faceless cowled monk has been seen here by a mother and daughter living in an old house there.

5. Ye Olde King's Head, Lower Bridge Street - A spectral child is said to haunt this old pub, in particular bedroom no. 6

6. Bookland, Bridge Street - This popular bookstore is said to be haunted by the ghost of a Victorian apprentice boy, who fell on stone steps at the back of the medieval crypt. The boy's spirit has also been experienced upstairs in the tea room.

7. Boot Inn, Eastgate Row North - This was once Chester's most notorious brothel. It is claimed by staff and customers that ghostly female moans and laughter occasionally resonate through the pub.

8. The Bingo Hall, Brook Street - An entity known as "Old George" is said to walk this building. Inexplicable thumps and crashes have been heard up in the attic, and a shape in a tweed jacket has been seen on the balcony, but vanishes when approached by anybody.

9. The Pied Bull, Northgate Street - Said to be one of the most haunted pubs in Britain, The Pied Bull was the subject of an investigation by the TV show *Whines and Spirits*, which is presented by *Most Haunted's* Karl Beattie and Stuart Torevell. Ghosts are said to haunt the 12 rooms, and the pub's cellar is said to be the spookiest place, with staff refusing to even venture down there!

True Ghost Stories

10. 13 Watergate Street - A typical example of a poltergeist haunting. Brushes, cards, kettles and glass vases all move by themselves, phenomena that has been experienced by various customers.

5. St. George's Hall

St George's Hall in Liverpool first opened its doors to the public in 1854, over 10 years after it was first commissioned. The architect responsible for the main design of the hall was a gentleman called Harvey Lonsdale Elmes.

The Hall was constructed to provide a suitable venue for the triennial music festivals. On top of this, the courts were added, as Elmes had been commissioned to design both buildings, and due to funding 'issues' they were combined.

Over the years, there have been many reports of paranormal occurrences at the hall. The condemned cells, the courtrooms, the lower floors and the air ducts, which were used by the hall's workers, have all been mentioned as areas where supernatural activity has happened. Many high profile cases have been heard in the courts over the years, and it is said that the old cells still feel the ghostly presences of all those convicted souls that were condemned to death.

Some guests of the building, while standing on the steps in the great hall, have felt cold hands touching them, and then felt themselves being pushed forward by some unknown entity. In the concert room, a man has been sighted sitting with his head in his hands. When asked by staff if he needs assistance, he just disappears into thin air. Other people have reported experiencing intense feelings of coldness whilst walking in various areas of the hall.

Down below in the basement, strange voices have been

True Ghost Stories

heard, and a presence of a tall gentleman shouting has been seen - supervising the workers, perhaps.

The hall was the subject of a big charity ghost hunt conducted by www.mosthaunted-ghosttours.com in March 2008.

St George's Hall was reopened on April 23rd 2007 by HRH The Prince of Wales, after the completion of a £23m restoration. The Hall has been carefully restored to its original glory and a new Heritage Centre has been created to provide visitors with a dynamic and exciting introduction to St George's Hall and its place in Liverpool's history.

6. The South Shields Poltergeist

In the summer of 2006, Darren W. Ritson was asked to investigate a "haunting" in an unassuming, ordinary terraced house in the town of South Shields, Tyne & Wear. Darren asked another veteran researcher, Michael J. Hallowell, to accompany him.

During the subsequent months the authors made literally dozens of visits to the house in question, and witnessed first-hand the malevolent, sadistic power of the poltergeist. It was an experience they would never forget.

Initially, the entity just tried to scare the family by moving various objects around the house and making mysterious banging noises - the kind of behaviour that has always been attributable to poltergeist activity. However, as the weeks went on, the entity's activity took on a more threatening and evil aspect. The following examples are just a few of the tactics employed by the South Shield's Poltergeist to intimidate both the family and the paranormal investigators:

1. Death threats sent to the mobile phone of one of the members of the experiments.

2. A toilet cistern filled with blood, which then mysteriously vanished.

3. Knives thrown at both the investigators and the experiments.

True Ghost Stories

4. Appearing as a malevolent, silhouette-type entity in front of both the experiments and the investigators.

5. Slashing the body of one of the experiments with dozens of cuts during filming.

6. Talking to investigators and TV reporters through a number of children's toys.

Eventually, thanks to the help of several experts from a number of different professional, forensic, academic and investigative backgrounds, the authors were able to terminate the reign of terror that the South Shields Poltergeist had wreaked - a reign of terror that had lasted for almost a whole year.

7. The Enfield Poltergeist

In 1977, a family who lived in a rented council house in Enfield, UK, began a terrifying ordeal when a Poltergeist took over their lives. The family consisted of divorcee Margaret (Peggy) Hodgson and her four children: Margaret aged 12, Janet 11, Johnny 10 and Billy 7.

Phenomena started when the two girls were in bed and a chest of drawers started shuffling forwards. Their mother went upstairs to see what the commotion was. The girls were told to get back into bed and stop messing about. With that, the chest of drawers suddenly lurched forwards. The mother pushed it back in place, only for the chest to immediately move forwards again! The family were kept awake all night long with strange noises and knockings. The following morning, exhausted, the family went into the neighbour's house and described the night's events. Vic Nottingham, the neighbour, went into the house to see if he could fathom what was going on. He too heard the noises, and says that the knocking followed him from room to room. This was the beginning of a yearlong period in which during the early stages, the family experienced more knocking on the walls, Lego bricks and marbles being thrown around aggressively, and more movement of furniture. It was later to take an even more terrifying turn, when a cast iron fireplace would be torn from the wall, fires would ignite and extinguish themselves spontaneously, and Janet would be thrown out of bed, and made to levitate. One of these incidents was witnessed by two passers by, who stopped in amazement to watch Janet levitating horizontally in her bedroom window, whilst toys were swirling around in the air behind her!

They were frightened out of their wits and the Mother was at such a loss of what to do that she called the police. When they arrived on the scene, they witnessed a chair lift up in the air, and then, as it came to rest, it shot 4ft forward across the floor. The police even wrote a statement to this effect. The newspapers were called and a senior reporter for the Daily Mirror went to interview the family. She also witnessed strange events. It was then suggested that paranormal investigators should be brought in. And so began an intensive study that was to last for many months with paranormal researchers, Maurice Grosse and Guy Lyon Playfair.

Maurice Grosse stated that the terror within the family was completely apparent. Desperate to help them, he would visit the family on an almost daily basis in order to offer support and to investigate the phenomena. During the latter months of this haunting, the phenomena took an unexpected twist when, one day, the family was in the living room and suddenly a dog started barking. But they didn't have a dog. Maurice decided that if the entity was able to produce a bark, perhaps it could be coaxed into speaking. He began asking questions and to his amazement the entity answered! The voice was strange, deep and guttural, and very much sounded like that of an old man. But the voice came from Janet! Examination showed that to produce such a sound, the voice would have to come from the false vocal cords situated deep in the throat. However, to speak in this way is painful and damaging, and to speak in this way for any length of time is said to be medically impossible. The voice was recorded on many occasions, and the girl, who was seemingly possessed, was made to take a sip of water and have her mouth taped up. After the voice was heard and recorded, she would be un-taped and would spit out the water. Interestingly, the voice claimed to be that of a man called Bill who said that he was the previous occupier of the house, and stated that he had died of a brain haemorrhage in an armchair in the living room. This was confirmed to be true, and when the tape was played to the man's son, the son was adamant that the voice was that of his Father.

There was a brief period where the two girls were thought to be hoaxing the phenomena. Indeed, they did admit to playing some tricks on Maurice. They state that they used to get fed up with being constantly tested like guinea pigs and wanted to see if he could catch them out, which he did every time! There is an extremely interesting film, titled 'Interview With A Poltergeist', which reconstructs these events. And many of the witnesses, including Maurice Grosse, the Daily Mirror reporter, the police, and the two daughters are interviewed. It's interesting to note the girls' accounts from their perspectives as adults. They are clearly still affected by what they went through. Their testaments leave very little doubt that their experiences were genuine.

8. The Whaley House

The Whaley House, situated in San Diego and replete with such a colourful history, is said to be the number one most haunted house in the United States. The spirits of the Whaley House have been reported on numerous paranormal television programs, and have been documented in countless publications and books since the house first opened as a museum in 1960.

The earliest reported ghost at the Whaley House is an entity called "Yankee Jim." James (aka Santiago) Robinson was convicted of attempted grand larceny in San Diego in 1852, and hanged on a gallows off the back of a wagon on the site where the house now stands. Although Thomas Whaley had watched the execution, he did not let it dissuade him from buying the property a few years later and building a family home there. According to the San Diego Union, "soon after the couple and their children moved in, heavy footsteps were heard moving about the house. Whaley described them as sounding as though they were made by the boots of a large man. He eventually concluded that these unexplained footfalls were made by Yankee Jim Robinson." Another source states that Lillian Whaley, the family's' youngest daughter who lived in the house until 1953, had been convinced the ghost of "Yankee Jim" haunted the Old House.

Many visitors to the house have reported encountering

Thomas Whaley himself. The late June Reading, former curator of the museum, said, "We had a little girl, perhaps 5 or 6 years old, who waved to a man she said was standing in the parlour. We couldn't see him. But often children's sensitivity is greater than an adult's." However, many adults have reported seeing the apparition of Mr. Whaley, usually on the upper landing. The spectre of Anna Whaley has also been reported, usually in the downstairs rooms or in the garden. In 1964, Mrs. Whaley's floating spirit even appeared to television personality Regis Philbin.

Other visitors have described experiencing the presence of a woman in the courtroom. "I see a small figure of a woman," one visitor said, "who has a swarthy complexion. She is wearing a long full skirt, reaching to the floor. She has a cap on her head, dark hair and eyes, and she is wearing gold hoops in her pierced ears." None of the Whaleys match this description, but the house was rented out to many tenants over the years, so maybe the mysterious woman in the courtroom was one of these.

Another presence reported is that of a young girl, who is usually seen in the dining room. Psychic Sybil Leek encountered this spirit during a visit in the 1960s. "It was a long-haired girl," Sybil said. "She was very quick, in a longish dress. She went to the table in this room and I went to the chair." This is said to be the ghost of a playmate of the Whaley children, who accidentally broke her neck on a low-hanging clothesline in the backyard, and whose name was either Annabel or Carrie Washburn. There are no historic records of any child dying this way at the Whaley House; nor is there record of any family named Washburn residing in San Diego at the time. Apparently this legend was started by a former employee of the Whaley House, possibly to add

True Ghost Stories

to the house's mystique.

Even animal ghosts have been seen. A parapsychologist reported he saw a spotted dog that ran down the hall with his ears flapping and into the dining room. The dog, he claimed, was an apparition. When they lived in the house, the Whaley's owned a terrier named Dolly Varden.

Every day, visitors come from all around the world to tour the historic museum. It contains so much history within its walls, that even the non-believer will enjoy the tour. For believers and sceptics alike, the house draws them back time and again, in search of those elusive ghosts.

9. Sexual Ghosts

Over the centuries, there have been many reported cases - especially in Medieval legend - of sexual hauntings involving two specific types of entities: the Incubus (male demon) and the Succubus (female demon).

The Incubus and Succubus usually manifest themselves during the nocturnal hours, preying on the victim when they are sleeping, although there have been some cases where females have actually been sexually assaulted whilst fully awake. One such experience was covered in the book and subsequent movie, The Entity.

Any female who undergoes an incubus sexual assault will not awaken, although she may experience it in a dream. If she becomes pregnant, the child will grow inside her as any normal child, except that it will possess supernatural powers. Usually the child grows into a person of evil character or a powerful wizard. According to legend, it is said that the magician Merlin was the result of physical contact between an incubus and a nun.

A succubus is the female version, and she seduces men. According to one legend, the incubus and the succubus were fallen angels. The word incubus is Latin for "nightmare". In medieval Europe, the succubus was a female demon (or evil spirit) who visits men in their sleep to lie with them in ghostly sexual intercourse. The man who falls victim to a succubus will not awaken, although may experience it whilst in the dream state. The biblical Lilith, the first wife to Adam before Eve, is said to also have been the very first succubus on earth. There is a version of the Lilith myth in every religion in the world. Many of these creatures have different names, such as Marilith or Lilitu, but all of them have one common theme: a demon woman, often with wings, who seduces - and sometimes murders - men. A succubus.

Just as is the case with the succubus, there are also many legends about incubi (singular: incubus), but these are not be confused with succubi (which is the plural of succubus). The incubi are said to be fallen angels in Judeo-Christianity who fell to earth because they had sex with mortal women. Since then incubi have stalked the earth, seducing women in their dreams and impregnating them. The children of incubi are said to grow up to become rapists.

An evil person who raped and murdered in real life may pass on, but may not move on to Heaven or Hell. Instead, they remain on the earth plane as a spiritual being with the same personality as they had in life. They are therefore free to indulge in sexual intercourse with whomever they chose, so it's not surprising that a spirit of such a nature may be called an Incubus or a Succubus. Many of these themes have been touched upon in books, or in a number of fantasy online games, or even in television.

There are many variations of this sexual demonic legend all over the world. For instance, in Zanzibar, an entity known as the "Popo Bawa" generally preys on men as they sleep in their beds. In the Chilo, Province of Chile, a pathetic little dwarf, known as El Trauco, woos young naive women and then seduces them. In Hungary, a Liderc is a demonic sexual predator that operates under the cover of darkness, and will appear as little more than a wispy apparition or a fiery light. Any one of these two succubi can be blamed for unexpected or unwanted pregnancies, especially in unmarried women, though you could argue that it might just be a convenient fabrication to avoid vicious gossip!

Some confuse the incubus with the legendary "Old Hag" syndrome, but it is not. The Old Hag episode is usually confined to a feeling of intense pressure on the chest and, as such, not an actual ghostly sexual encounter. Another difference that separates the incubus/succubus experience from the Old Hag is that the former is not always unpleasant while the Old Hag is mostly accompanied by a feeling of death, suffocation and the horrific feeling of fighting for your life.

Because the incubus and succubus are generally experienced during the sleep state or in between it, most experts feel that it is an imaginary experience and not a real one. However, telling this to the person who has just had this eerily erotic experience, they may find that hard to believe, as to them it feels as real as actual sexual intercourse itself.

Nobody can really say for sure if these events are real or imagined, but until you've experienced an actual sexual assault by an incubus or succubus yourself, it's quite hard to form a solid opinion one way or the other.

10. The Amityville Horror

The Amityville Horror is one of the most documented and well-known cases of a haunted house in the history of paranormal research.

The story - which was alleged to have happened to the Lutz family when they moved into a large Dutch colonial house at 112 Ocean Avenue in Amityville - has been the subject of a series of best-selling books and a string of movies.

When George and Kathy Lutz, along with Kathy's three children, first moved into their new house in Amityville on December 18th, 1975, they thought they had found their dream home. It was near the school, suiting the kids well, and the neighbours seemed friendly enough, with Kathy even envisioning herself enjoying sociable casino poker games with them. That is, of course, until that dream became a living nightmare, as they started experiencing the strange paranormal occurrences which eventually drove them out of the house.

Prior to the Lutzes' occupation of the Amityville house, the residence had been the scene of a horrific murder spree. On November 13th, 1974, 23-year-old Ronald DeFeo shot dead his father, mother and four younger siblings. However, not being superstitious, the Lutz's still bought the house.

By January 14th, 1976, when the Lutzes fled the house forever, they claimed to have been terrorised for 28 days by an unspeakably evil entity. Their horrific experiences included ghostly apparitions of hooded figures, swarms of flies in the sewing room and the children's playroom, breaking window panes, spine-chilling cold alternating with suffocating heat, personality changes, nightly parades by spirit marching bands, levitations, green slime oozing down the stairs, foul odours, nausea, inexplicable scratches on Kathleen's body, objects mysteriously moving, constant disconnection of the telephone service, and even communications between the youngest, Melissa, and a devilish spirit pig by the name of "Jodie".

But more shockingly, even the Devil himself is said to have actually appeared in the house.

Even visitors to the house were affected by the strange atmosphere permeating through the place. Kathy's brother, Jimmy, and his new bride mysteriously lost $1,500 in cash. And Father Mancuso, the local priest who gave the house his blessing, suffered a horrible bout of sickness that left him physically drained. As a result, he eventually transferred to a distant parish. He is said to have heard a voice from an unseen entity ordering him to "get out" when he sprinkled the house with holy water.

In 1977, The Amityville Horror by Jay Anson was published. The book became an instant bestseller, and led to a top-grossing movie in 1979, starring James Brolin and Margot Kidder. More Amityville Horror books followed, written by different authors, which gave alleged accounts of the demonic entity still following the Lutzes, even after they had fled the Amityville house.

As is often the norm with cases like this, many sceptics claimed that the Amityville haunting was just a big hoax, and they were quick to point out various discrepancies in

Anson's book. Even Jerry Solfvin, of the Psychical Research Foundation, who was contacted by George Lutz in early January 1976 about paranormal activity at the house, found the whole case rather questionable. All the evidence was subjective. Also, Father Mancuso was regarded as being a poor witness, as he had visited the house only the once. It took Anson three or four months to write his book, and he worked mostly from tapes of telephone interviews. Apparently, he made only a superficial effort to verify the Lutzes' account.

The most significant aspect of the case is the interview that Ronald DeFeo's lawyer, William Weber, gave a local radio station in 1979. He claimed that the Lutzes concocted the whole Amityville Horror saga around their kitchen table whilst drinking bottles of wine. He also said that after approaching them with the idea, the Lutzes broke away from him, and so he decided to sue for his share of the book and movie royalties. But the Lutzes counter sued, arguing that their experiences were genuine. Mrs Lutz's story was later analysed on a Psychological Stress Evaluation. The results of the test confirmed her claims.

Although it's possible that the hauntings at the Amityville residence may have actually happened, many observers have deemed the Lutzes' story to be over-dramatic when compared to other cases of paranormal activity.

11. Harry Price

Harry Price is probably the most famous name in the world of ghost hunting. The investigation he is most noted for is that of the haunting at Borley Rectory, dubbed "The most haunted house in England." In the 1930s and 1940s, Price contributed many articles on ghosts and the paranormal to various newspapers and magazines.

Contrary to what many people think, Price certainly wasn't a psychic researcher in the modern sense, but an investigative journalist who specialised in debunking fraudulent mediums and similar charlatans. He claimed to be a scientist, but actually had no training in the scientific field. After gathering some hunting supplies and being in the field and feeling out your equipment, you will steadily become a much better hunter.

Harry Price was born on the 17th January 1881 in Red Lion Square, London. He was educated in London at Waller Road School and Haberdashers' Aske's Hatcham College, the Haberdashers' Aske's Hatcham Boys School. At the age of 15, Price founded the Carlton Dramatic Society and wrote small plays, including a drama about his early experience with a poltergeist. which he said took place at a haunted manor house in Shropshire.

Price was also a keen coin collector, and wrote several articles for The Askean, the magazine for Haberdashers' School. In his autobiography, Search for Truth, written between 1941 and 1942, Price claimed he was involved with archaeological excavations in Greenwich Park, London, but in earlier writings on Greenwich denied he had a hand in the excavation. From May 1908, Price continued his interest in archaeology at Pulborough, Sussex, where he had moved to before marrying Constance Mary Knight that August. As well as working for paper merchants Edward Saunders & Sons as a salesman, he wrote for two local Sussex newspapers about his remarkable propensity for discovering 'clean' antiquities.

In his autobiography, Search for Truth, Price said the "Great Sequah" in Shrewsbury was "entirely responsible for shaping much of my life's work", and led to him acquiring the first volume of what would become the Harry Price Library, Price later became an expert amateur conjurer, joined the Magic Circle in 1922 and maintained a lifelong interest in stage magic and conjuring. His expertise in sleight-of-hand and magic tricks stood him in good stead for what would become his all consuming passion: the investigation of paranormal phenomena.

Price's first major success in psychical research came in 1922, when he exposed the 'spirit' photographer William Hope. The following year, Price made a formal offer to the University of London to equip and endow a Department of Psychical Research, and to loan the equipment of the National Laboratory and its library. The University of London Board of Studies in Psychology responded positively to this proposal and, in 1934, the University of London Council for Psychical Investigation was formed with Price as Honorary Secretary and Editor. In the meanwhile, in 1927, Price joined the Ghost Club, of which he remained a member until it (temporarily) closed in 1936.

Alan Toner

In 1934, the National Laboratory of Psychical Research took on its most illustrious case. £50 was paid to the medium Helen Duncan so that she could be examined under scientific conditions. A sample of Helen Duncan's ectoplasm had been previously examined by the Laboratory and found to be largely made of egg white. Price found that Duncan's spirit manifestations were cheesecloth that had been swallowed and regurgitated by Duncan. Price later wrote up the case in Leaves from a Psychic's Case Book in a chapter called "The Cheese-cloth Worshippers". During Duncan's famous trial in 1944, Price gave his results as evidence for the prosecution.

Price's psychical research continued with investigations into Karachi's Indian rope trick and the fire-walking abilities of Kuda Bux in1935. He was also involved in the formation of the National Film Library, becoming its first chairman, and was a founding member of the Shakespeare Film Society. In 1936 Price made the first ever "live" broadcast from a supposedly haunted manor house in Meopham, Kent, for the BBC, and published The Confessions of a Ghost-Hunter and The Haunting of Cashen's Gap. This year also saw the transfer of Price's library on permanent loan to the University of London, followed shortly by the laboratory and investigative equipment. In 1937, he conducted further televised experiments into fire walking with Ahmed Hussain at Carshalton and Alexandra Palace, and also rented Borley Rectory for one year. The following year, Price re-established the Ghost Club, with himself as chairman, modernizing it and changing it from a spiritualist association to a group of open-minded sceptics that met to discuss paranormal topics. He was also the first to admit women to the club.

True Ghost Stories

In the same year, Price conducted experiments with Rahman Bey, who was 'buried alive' in Carshalton, and drafted a Bill for the regulation of psychic practitioners. In 1939, he organized a national telepathic test in the periodical John O'London's Weekly. During the 1940s, Price concentrated on writing and published three works: The Most Haunted House in England, Poltergeist Over England and The End of Borley Rectory.

In December 2008, an original unpublished 26-page manuscript by British writer Marjorie Bowen (1885-1952) attacking Price's investigation of the Borley Rectory case, was featured on an eBay auction.

Even though Price was a dedicated and meticulous paranormal investigator, and cultivated a leading reputation in the world of ghost hunting, he did generate much controversy in regard to just how genuine his investigations were, and that controversy continues even to this day. For instance, many have accused him of faking ghostly activity, especially in regard to his most famous investigation at Borley Rectory. Also, a photograph of Price and a spirit taken by William Hope was later proven to be a fake.

Some people have often asked the question: Does serious scientific research and a publicity-hungry ghost hunter go together? There have been arguments that Price had compromised his research into the paranormal with his penchant for highlight and spectacle. Even so, he did take psychical research out of the cold laboratory and dusty parlour séance room and gave it to an eager public. Price often displayed contrasting tendencies: a committed paranormal investigator and father of British ghost hunting, yet also a man who knew the value of a good ghost story when he saw one. If he has a legacy it is indeed programmes

Alan Toner

such as Most Haunted, Ghost Hunters and The World's Most Scariest Places. On the surface, serious paranormal research, but underneath, edge-of-seat, sheer spooky entertainment.

12. Ghosts of The Titanic

We all know the most tragic maritime story of all time: the sinking of the Titanic by an iceberg in the North Atlantic Ocean on April 14th, 1912. However, what many of us may not know is that, over the years, there have been many strange stories centred around the ill-fated ship. The most reported story has been that involving the Titanic Exhibit, which is housed in the Georgia Museum, and which travels from one major city to the next, giving people the opportunity to view many of the once-lost artefacts from the monumental wreckage. The exhibit is reported to be haunted.

Ghostly apparitions, disembodied voices and strange footsteps have been reported at many locations on the Titanic exhibit tour, and volunteers who work at the exhibit claim to have experienced an eerie presence around them while walking through the artefacts. These reports cannot be so easily dismissed, for it is quite often the case that spirits do attach themselves to certain artefacts, and haunt whatever location houses them. This could well be the case with the Titanic, for obviously, unlike haunted properties, it is no longer actually standing, but has left behind many artefacts which could quite easily have been left with supernatural potential.

It is not known for sure just how many ghosts haunt the Titanic Exhibition. More than 1,500 people went down with the ship on that fateful evening of April 14th, 1912, so it could be any one or any number of those deceased souls.

A spokeswoman for the aquarium, Meghann Gibbons, has expressed her belief, and the belief of many volunteers working on the exhibit, that it is in fact haunted. One visitor to the Titanic Exhibit, with her daughter and 4-year-old grandson, firmly agree. According to her story, while viewing the 1st class quarters, she and her daughter thought little of the young boy's repeated questioning, "Who is that lady?" and "What is she doing?" They assured him that there was only a dress laid out over the love seat, as if waiting to be adorned. It wasn't until they heard later that the TAPS ghost hunting team was investigating paranormal activity in the Titanic Exhibit that they believed the boy had experienced his first ghostly encounter.

Many visitors to the exhibit claimed to have experienced an eerie feeling, as if being watched, or feeling an immense sadness around specific objects or areas of the exhibit. Most assumed it was a general sombre mood evoked by the 1912 disaster, but as more and more reports come in with similar claims, a lot of people are starting to give these reports credence - including the TAPS team of paranormal investigators from Sci-Fi's "Ghost Hunters". The TAPS lead investigators, Jay and Grant, strongly believe that the Titanic Exhibit is haunted. After a lengthy investigation, which aired on the 97th anniversary of the ship's tragic demise, the TAPS team found sufficient evidence of paranormal activity, including an eerie EVP recording. They were seated in a room trying to communicate with the ghost, and asked the spirit if it wanted them to leave. The voice distinctly replied, "Now - please, wait." Unfortunately, Jay and Grant could not follow up on the questions, since they did not hear the voice until later, when the evidence was being analysed.

This year (2012), a group of ghost hunters plan to mark the 100th anniversary of the Titanic's sinking by travelling out to the exact location of the ship's sinking and searching for any residual impressions left behind from the incident. The group, appropriately named D.E.A.D (direct, evidence, after, death), hope to achieve results mainly from the use of sophisticated EVP recorders. Their spokesperson, William Brower, says they will be recreating the atmosphere of the doomed Titanic's last hours by serving up the same meals and listening to the same type of music heard on that fateful night a century ago. One of the group, Angelica Harris, hopes this will be a fitting tribute to those that died, including her great uncle who was aboard.

The supernatural incidents revolving around the Titanic could be attributable to residual impressions, which are often left behind after an event of extreme trauma, like the emotional trauma experienced by all those people who went down with the Titanic. Will the group pick up sounds of those who died, desperately screaming out for help in the icy waters of the North Atlantic Ocean? Only time will tell.

13. Haunted Shops and Stores

Old houses and ancient, crumbling castles are not the only places where ghosts have been reported. Over the years, there have also been many cases of spirits haunting major department stores, and even corner shops.

A few years ago, my mum worked in a confectioners in Birkenhead. With it being a very old shop, it was said to have a resident ghost. My mum soon found out that the stories were true. One day, when she was serving in the shop, two old ladies came in, and they walked up to the end of the counter to look at the cakes on display. My mum was at the other end at the till. On top of the counter was a large straw tray, which was used to display packets of batches. As the other assistant was taking hot pasties out of the oven, my mum had just finished serving a customer and was putting the money into the till when suddenly, without any visible cause whatsoever, the tray got lifted up off the counter and thrown at her shoulder. The tray then crashed to the floor and all the packets of batches fell onto the floor. The two old ladies that were in the shop looked on in utter shock and disbelief, and declared that it wasn't them as they were standing at the other end of the shop. Furthermore, my mum's work colleague said that she too had witnessed what had happened, and shook her head in disbelief also. My mum had no explanation for this strange incident, but it was just one of many more incidents she experienced in the shop, including serviettes flying around in the air after they had all been neatly put in the window, crisp packets getting dropped on the floor on their own, and different items mysteriously going missing.

One of the creepiest incidents in this cake shop happened to the manageress, who told the story to my mum. She used to go to the shop early in the morning to prepare everything for the opening at nine o'clock. As she was putting the trays of cakes into the racks, ready to put on small trays later, she had a feeling she was being watched. She looked over her shoulder . . . and there, standing in the doorway of the shop, was a tall, handsome, young man, dressed in a boiler suit, and he just stood there, staring at her silently. Her immediate thought was that it was a customer, so she told him to hang on a minute while she finished putting the cakes into the racks. When she turned back around a few seconds later, the man had vanished. She then went cold as she realised something: how could this man possibly have entered the shop, when the door was locked? Thinking that he might have gained access through the back entry, she went out there to check, but discovered that the padlocks were all still on the door. Again, she could not explain this incident, and therefore decided that it must have been a spirit.

The Toys 'R' Us store in Sunnyvale, California, has a long history of being haunted by a ghost called "Johnny Johnston," said to be a disappointed lover who bled to death after a farm accident, and store workers have reported seeing strange things happening, such as rag dolls and toy trucks leaping off shelves, balls bouncing down the aisles, children's books falling out of racks, and baby swings moving on their own. The shop's staff have tried to find a logical explanation for all these incidents, but just can't. The store has been featured on the TV show That's Incredible and other programmes. A Hollywood scriptwriter for the movie Toys spent two nights there doing research. Psychic Sylvia Browne held a séance in the store in 1978 and has since been back a few times.

An Asda store in Pwllheli is said to be haunted by the ghost of a long-haired man in a trench coat. The apparition has often been seen by staff in various parts of the store.

The Marks & Spencer store in Church Street, Liverpool, is said to be haunted by the ghost of a woman from the 1930's called "Lulu". This spirit often appears on the top floors of the store, and she carries a soda siphon, which she has occasionally squirted at people! The other ghost said to haunt the store is that of a man called Billy McMullen, a 22-year-old junior porter who suffered a tragic violent death at the Compton Hotel (the building that once occupied the site) in March 1877, after fooling around in the hotel's lift.

Another Liverpool retail site, which has garnered something of a reputation for ghostly activity, is the old Owen Owen building, which now houses Tesco Metro. Back in the 1970's, an Owen Owen female sales assistant saw a tall distinguished-looking gentleman dressed in Victorian clothing as she worked in an upstairs room. In another incident, a young man serving in one of the departments saw and felt a hand on his shoulder. As he turned around, he was shocked to see that the hand had no arm or body attached. A customer also witnessed this eerie apparition. When a medium visited the Owen Owen store soon after it closed, she determined that there were at least seven spirits haunting the building, all from different eras. A security guard also had a strange experience whilst working there during a refurbishment prior to occupation by another firm. He soon discovered the place was haunted when he did his rounds. On one occasion, the security officer found a strange pair of scissors lying on the floor, and when he examined them, they looked blackened and quite old. He put them in his rucksack, but the next morning, when he reached home, the scissors had mysteriously vanished. The guard and some of his workmates used the Ouija board at the haunted building one night, and a word that the men didn't understand came through: **GORSUCH**. The guards laughed at the word. They didn't know that in the 19th century, a barber named John Gorsuch had his premises on Parker Street. This would probably explain the scissors that had appeared in the building.

In Hereford, there have been quite a few retail stores where ghostly activity has been witnessed. For instance, at the Sainsbury's store (a very modern building which, as such, would be the last place you would expect to be haunted), the ghost of an old lady has been seen many times by staff. She does a lot of waving and smiling at people. One morning, at 4am, a member of staff came in to open the store, and he saw the old lady as he was unlocking the fire exits. The old lady was standing there waving at him, her appearance so clear that the man waved back thinking it was a customer - only to suddenly realize that it was 4 am in the morning and no one was in there shopping! When the man approached the lady to ask her to leave the store, she simply disappeared into thin air. A similar story was when the manager once saw the old lady in the periphery of her vision. The manager asked her to go and do something, under the misconception that it was just a member of staff. After this, a member of staff popped her head around the corner and asked the manager who was she speaking to. The manager looked to where she saw the old lady, only to find that she had vanished. The staff who work in Sainsbury's say that there is a presence and a feeling of being watched. However, the ghost does seem to be a nice, friendly spirit. Sainsbury's supermarket was built on the old Barton Railway Station. In 1934, a G. V Bennett was in charge. The station was used for goods as well.

The Boots store, situated on Hereford's High Street, has some ghost stories that are very creepy. One evening, when the shop was empty, somebody saw a dark figure in the basement. On another occasion, there were two members of staff in the building, and they witnessed the fire drill being set off by unseen hands. The store was checked immediately, but no one else was present in the building at the time of the incident. If ghostly activity is really behind these incidents, then it is not surprising as the building has been around for many years and has had different uses. In 1879 this building was two different shops: a Thomas Frederick Hawkins was a Printer and Stationer, and a Mrs. Harriet Reeves was a Watchmaker. The place was also occupied by Marks and Spencer in 1934.

The Primark store, situated on Hereford's busy Widemarsh Street, has crowds of customers shopping there daily. But for a building that is so modern, it really is surprising to find a ghost story and so much history here. The building is known to stand on the site of where the Black Swan hotel previously was. A graveyard previously occupied the site before the Black Swan was built. The store itself is very large, and the front of the shop is said to be the oldest part. The old Co-op store was previously at this part of the store, Above is the stock room and cash office, and it is in these two rooms that the ghost of a smartly dressed man has been seen wandering around on numerous occasions. The staff has christened him "Freddie," and he has been sighted wearing a blue shirt and trousers. One member of staff who had a first hand account of the ghost was so upset and traumatised by her encounter that she left her job altogether. It is also believed that this ghostly man travels through the shops next to Primark. The Paperway shop, which is one shop down, also has a ghostly man in their shop who occasionally visits, and he is seen wearing the same clothing. The man could be from the old co-op store, as the staff uniform was blue. The dress shop, one door away from Primark on the left, also has a ghost of a man in the basement, so it could be that the same ghost is travelling in between all three of these shops. When the site was the Black Swan hotel, it had a reputation of being one of the city's best pubs, and coaches left the inn daily, travelling to Liverpool, in 1834. The inn had many landlords over duration. Thomas Jones was victualler in 1822, and in 1909 a Thomas Owen was head of the inn. The Black Swan also had air raid shelters provided in the basement.

Thornton's chocolate shop in Eastgate Street, Chester, is said to be haunted by a ghost called Sarah, who hung herself after being jilted on her wedding day. Sarah wreaks most of her unearthly havoc in the top floor front room and in the cellar. However, her ghost has also manifested in other parts of the shop. Although she is never seen, she has been heard coming down the stairs singing a strange song and holding out her hands, as if lifting up a long dress to facilitate her descent. She once pushed an American tourist down the stairs. She once frightened an electrician who came to read the meter in the cellar. During Valentine's Day 1991, Sarah got upset over the display in the shop and scattered the heart-shaped boxes of chocolates all over the floor. However, the ordinary boxes of chocolates were left undisturbed. An exorcism held in 1965 dispelled Sarah's poltergeist-like antics for a while. However, she has apparently returned, and still creates ghostly disturbances in the shop right to this day.

14. The Fleece Inn

The Fleece Inn, situated in the market town of Elland in Yorkshire, is said to be home to many different kinds of ghosts from many centuries. Built in the early 17th Century, it was originally a farmhouse called The Great House Farm.

The building has a long history of crime, as several murders have been committed there over the centuries, and the ghosts of many of these unfortunate victims and their evil murderers are said to still haunt the Fleece Inn even to this day.

The Fleece Inn incurred a notorious reputation for attracting prostitutes, who would often solicit for clients in the pub, in the hope that the alcohol would stimulate the progress of their business. One of these prostitutes, who was pregnant when she died, is said to have been slaughtered there with an axe. There is also the case of a servant girl who was viciously assaulted and pushed down the stairs to her death. Her ghost is said to haunt the spot where she met her death. The Fleece Inn's most famous ghost is Leathery Coits. This entity is reported to travel at great speed past the building, minus his head and in a coach drawn by headless horses. There is also the tale of a visitor to the Elland market at the start of the 19th Century, who died at the hands of a local man with whom he got into a fight. The bloodstained handprint of the murdered man remained on the stairs for over a hundred years, during which no amount of scrubbing or washing could remove it. It was eventually destroyed when the inn was renovated in the 1970s.

There have been many other strange entities seen moving around the Fleece Inn. However, in addition to the rather sinister spirits, there have also been many benign ghosts. For instance, when the inn was a farmhouse, the spirit of a farmer called Will is reported to sit in a chair near the fireplace. In life, this man would have probably loved coming in, removing his boots and just relaxing there in his chair, after his laborious work all day out in the fields. His presence has been sensed many times. There are also two other former inhabitants whose spirits are said to walk the inn: Alice Pollard and William Wooler. Both were landlords in the 1800s.

There have also been strange olfactory happenings in the inn. The delicious smell of freshly baked bread has been smelt in an area that was once the kitchen. An aroma of lemon has also been sensed, which permeates the air quite suddenly and from an unknown source.

The ghost of a young girl called Jane has been heard running up and down the stairs and through the rooms, giggling constantly as she goes. There have also been many reports of strange voices and running footsteps in the upper rooms of the building. In addition, a weird banging noise has been heard throughout the building.

The Fleece Inn has long been described as having a rather oppressive aura about it, and many people have experienced intense feelings of sadness there, as they want to break down and cry. Others have reported feelings of intoxication, even though they've had no drink. This could be attributable to the fact that the inn has obviously seen more than its fair share of drunkards over the years.

15. Interactive Ghosts

Interactive ghosts are so called because they always purposely make their presence known to people. They communicate with the physical world by sending messages, and often the spirit is seen only by the recipient of the message.

The ghost is usually well known to the person - either a relative or a friend - and might predict some imminent news, like a birth or a death. Such a message is relayed by the ghost actually speaking to the recipient, or by some other method, such as making some kind of noise.

You might think that all this is solid proof that such ghosts really do exist, but the chance of such dreams or predictions really happening is actually much higher than you might think. For instance, many is the time that somebody has imagined a happy event - like a birth or an engagement - and if that person subsequently dreams of this event, only to be told the next day that you are about to become an uncle or aunt, does that necessarily make you feel that you have some kind of inherent psychic power? It could be attributed to just sheer coincidence. The chances could be quite high of any one person in a large town having a predictive dream on a particular day.

But there is a difference here in regard to interactive ghosts: they always appear to the witness while he or she is fully awake. This begs the question: why does the spirit choose to appear only to one particular person?

If you take the example of deathbed messages - which have been reported many times throughout history - you could say that these are the work of an interactive ghost. In such circumstances, the apparition appears only at the time of trauma, and not some time afterwards.

There have also been many cases, over the years, of out-of-the-body experiences. During such incidents, the person concerned has found their 'spirit' floating up towards the ceiling and looking down on their apparently lifeless body. The hospital files are full of such reports of patients who have "temporarily died." These experiences usually occur when the person is in a traumatic condition, such as being close to death. When the person's spirit returns to their body, they often describe, in stunningly accurate detail, everything that was happening around them - even things taking place in rooms next door.

The phantom hitchhiker is another type of interactive ghost. These entities usually haunt quiet country roads, and are often seen by motorists as they drive along late at night. Resurrection Mary, who is said to haunt the lonely country lanes near Chicago, is the most famous roadside ghost of all. Drivers have reported that when they have stopped the car to avoid hitting the figure, it then mysteriously vanishes. On other occasions, when the motorist has stopped to give the figure a lift, it suddenly disappears completely from out of the car. These spectral hitchhikers are therefore a classic example of interactive ghosts, as they respond to the observer in quite a physical, realistic way.

16. The Ghosts of Charles Dickens

Charles Dickens (1812-1870) is best known for his classic novels like Oliver Twist, David Copperfield and A Tale of Two Cities. But he is also fondly remembered for writing quite a few ghost stories. His most famous ghost story of all, of course, is A Christmas Carol (1843), featuring the tale of miserly old Ebenezer Scrooge, who is chastened towards a more benevolent nature by the visitation of three ghosts on Christmas Eve.

Unlike his more lengthy works, Dickens's ghost stories - often written quite swiftly - tend to be less hyperbolic and hardly meticulously plotted, but more limited in style, and less enriched with dramatic detail. He frequently published his ghost stories in Households Words and All The Year Round.

Dickens always regarded ghost stories as especially suitable for telling around the Christmas period. We all know how hugely successful - and so unforgettable - A Christmas Carol was. His other outstanding ghost story, "The Haunted Man and The Ghost's Bargain" (1848), is a fascinating piece of work. In this tale, a ghost bestows the gift of forgetting all past grievances, and those affected find their memory loss makes them inhuman, without limits to other people and without ability to forgive. Dickens was always keen to encourage other writers to produce stories of the supernatural for the Yuletide season.

Dickens's usual type of ghost story, devoid of all humour and any great concentration on moral reasoning, were written for the Christmas extra issues of 1865 and 1866. In "The Trial for Murder", the spirit of a murdered man appears to one of the jurors to ensure that the killer is punished. In "The Signal Man" (which is a popular Dickens tale in the "A Ghost Story for Christmas" TV series, often shown at Christmas time), a railway worker in a desolate station keeps seeing a phantom warning him of fatal accidents which are about to occur on the line.

Dickens had always held a strong fascination for the supernatural, although he did have some scepticism. A few of his stories actually ridiculed the paranormal. For instance, in "The Lawyer and The Ghost", a story that runs through The Pickwick Papers (1836-1837), a ghost is asked why he haunts a place that makes him so depressed when he could go somewhere more comfortable with better weather. And in "The Haunted House" (1859), a man who receives spirit messages is sent misspelt homilies. And in "Well Authenticated Rappings", incredible visitations are traced to hangovers and heartburn. Yet despite this touch of cynicism, Dickens claimed to have seen his dead mother and beloved sister-in-law, Mary, in a night vision that was something much than just a dream. He also wrote about seeing an apparition of his father (who was then still alive) standing by his bed early in the morning. When he reached out to touch his father's shoulder, the apparition vanished.

Dickens published the "Four Ghost Stories" in 1861, and one of them was the story of an artist who paints a dead girl's portrait after seeing her ghost. Dickens then received a letter

True Ghost Stories

from a painter who claimed that the incident had actually happened to him. Dickens then published the man's own story in the next issue of his magazine. In letters that Dickens subsequently wrote to his acquaintances, it was quite clear that he believed the painter's story.

In "The Uncommercial Traveller" (1860), Dickens wrote that the spooky stories related to him in childhood by his nurse had had a lasting effect. Certain critics have recognised a direct link between Dickens's later work and the stories told by the nurse. Dickens himself also stated that these tales "acquired an air of authentication that impaired my digestive powers for life."

Despite Dickens's reservations about the actual existence of ghosts, there is no doubt that when it came to telling a real good ghost story - especially those centred around a snowy Christmas atmosphere - he certainly knew how to entertain, and spook, his readers.

17. The Ghosts of Pluckley Village

Pluckley Village, in Kent, is said to be the most haunted village in the UK. Over the years, many kinds of spirits have been seen by both locals and tourists.

The ghost of an old gypsy, wrapped in a shawl and smoking a pipe, has often been spotted standing near a bridge. The shattered remains of an old oak tree, situated nearby, are a noted haunt for the apparition of a murdered highwayman. In life, the highwayman was said to have been killed by a sword, and it was this weapon that impaled him to the tree.

There are many buildings in Pluckley Village which are also reputed to be haunted. For instance, in the Church of Saint Nicholas, the spirit of Lady Dering, who was buried in three lead coffins to prevent her decay, occasionally manifests itself. She has been seen walking through the churchyard at night with the red rose, with which she was buried, unwithered on her breast. In the Dering Chapel, mysterious lights have been seen through its windows, and the disembodied voice of a woman has been heard in the churchyard. The spirit of a long-dead monk is said to haunt a house called Greystones, and the voice of a former owner of another house, Rose Court, has often been heard there as she calls her dogs. Also, the old mill is haunted by the ghost of a miller, who is said to be in constant search of his lost love during the nocturnal hours. In the Dering Arms public house, a spectral woman dressed in Victorian clothing hangs around the bar. In another pub, The Black Horse, a spectral hand moves items across the bar, tidies up, and occasionally hides coats and wallets. A ghostly carriage, pulled by two horses, has often been seen trotting down the main public street of Pluckley. The origin of this carriage is unknown.

But the most terrifying of all the entities said to haunt Pluckley Village has to be that of the so-called "Screaming Ghost". The blood curdling screams of this ghost have been heard in the area around the Brickworks, Pluckley Heath.

18. The Winchester House

The Winchester Mystery House is a well-known mansion in Northern California. Its name comes up quite often whenever there are discussions about the most haunted buildings in America. It is located at 525 South Winchester Blvd. in San Jose, California. It was once the personal residence of Sarah Winchester, the widow of gun magnate William Wirt Winchester. It was continuously under construction for 38 years and is said to be haunted by various entities. Some psychics have said that there are actually a total of three spirits currently residing in the mansion.

Under Winchester's supervision, its construction proceeded around the clock, without interruption, from 1884 until her death on September 5, 1922, when work immediately ceased. The cost for such constant building has been estimated at about US $5.5 million.

The Queen Anne Style Victorian mansion is famous for its sheer size and utter lack of a proper construction plan. In fact, many rooms in the house lead to dead ends. The miles of twisting hallways are made even more intriguing by secret passageways in the walls. Mrs. Winchester travelled through her house in a roundabout fashion, supposedly to confuse any mischievous ghosts that might be following her. According to popular belief, Winchester believed that the house was haunted by the ghosts of the people who were killed by Winchester rifles, and that only continuous construction would appease them.

The Boston Medium consulted by Mrs. Winchester explained that her family and her fortune were being haunted by the spirits of American Indians, Civil War soldiers, and others killed by Winchester rifles. Supposedly, the untimely deaths of her daughter and husband were caused by these spirits, and it was implied that Mrs. Winchester might be the next victim. However, the medium also claimed that there was an alternative: Mrs. Winchester could move west and appease the spirits by building a great house for them. As long as construction of the house never ceased, Mrs. Winchester could feel secure in the knowledge that her life was not in danger. Building such a house was even supposed to bring her eternal life. On a more practical note, maybe a change of scenery and a constant hobby were just what Mrs. Winchester needed to alleviate her grief.

Whatever her actual motivations, Mrs. Winchester packed her bags and left Connecticut to visit a niece who lived in Menlo Park, California. While there, she discovered the perfect spot for her new home in the Santa Clara Valley. In 1884 she purchased an unfinished farm house just three miles west of San Jose - and over the next thirty-eight years she produced the sprawling complex we know today as the Winchester Mystery House.

The Winchester House is now a popular tourist attraction. It has also been the subject of investigation by a number of TV paranormal shows. The house is owned by Winchester Investments LLC, and it retains unique touches that reflect Mrs Winchester's beliefs and her preoccupation with warding off malevolent spirits. These spirits are said to have directly influenced her as to exactly how the house should be built.

Fright Nights is a specifically ticketed special night time event at the Winchester Mystery House. On select nights in September and October, Winchester Mystery House is transformed into San Jose's most terrifying Halloween experience, filled with haunted walk-through attractions, intense scares, roaming scare actors, and nightmare inducing tales.

Since Mrs. Winchester's death, hundreds of fascinating stories have appeared about this mysterious woman and her sprawling mansion. It seems odd that neither her relatives nor her former employees ever contradicted these stories, despite that fact that some of them lived more than forty years after Mrs. Winchester's death. Did they feel threatened by talking – or did they deem it necessary to protect Mrs. Winchester's privacy, even after her death?

19. Ordsall Hall

Ordsall Hall is a historic house and a former stately home in Ordsall, Salford, Greater Manchester. It dates back over 750 years, although the oldest surviving parts of the present hall were built in the 15th century. The most important period of Ordsall Hall's life was as the family seat of the Radclyffe family, who lived in the house for over 300 years. The hall was the setting for William Harrison Ainsworth's 1842 novel Guy Fawkes, written around the plausible although unsubstantiated local story that the Gunpowder Plot of 1605 was planned in the house.

Like many old buildings, Ordsall Hall has gained a reputation over the years for being haunted. One of its many resident ghosts is a spirit called The White Lady, who is said to appear in the Great Hall or Star Chamber, This entity is said to be the ghost of Margaret Radclyffe, who died of a broken heart in 1599 following the death at sea of her twin, Alexander. The ghost of a little girl has also been seen, standing near the bottom of the stairs. There are web cams overseeing the areas that are said to be the most haunted. An episode of the television programme Most Haunted was filmed in the hall in 2004

Since its sale by the Radclyffes in 1662, the hall has been put to many uses: working men's club, school for clergy, and a radio station amongst them. The house was bought by Salford City Council in 1959, and opened to the public in

Alan Toner

1972, as a period house and local history museum. The hall is a Grade I listed building. In 2007 it was named Small Visitor Attraction of the Year by the Northwest Regional Development Agency. The hall was closed to the public between 2009 and 2011 while it was refurbished and reopened in May 2011.

20. The Ancient Ram Inn

The Ancient Ram Inn is a Grade II* listed building. and a former pub located in Wotton-under-Edge, a market town within the Stroud district of Gloucestershire, England. It is believed to be one of the most haunted hotels in the country. This famous inn is owned by and the home to John Humphries. It has been owned by many people since 1145 to present date. Many people lived here either as a tenant or overnight guests. This inn was said to have also been owned by the local St. Mary's Church when first built.

The paranormal phenomena reported to have manifested in the Inn include spectral shadows, strange footsteps, inexplicable drops in temperature, mysterious tapping sounds, strange orbs of flight floating around the Inn after dark, furniture being moved around, and people being pushed to the ground by an unseen force.

The owner, John Humphries, even claims to have been a victim of an incubus assault. And the Inn is said to have not one ghost but several - including a phantom cavalier, a witch, a man and a monk. There have also been sightings of a mysterious black cat. The fact that the Inn was built on an ancient pagan burial ground may have something to do with all the ghostly activity that has occurred there over the years.

What is particularly scary about the hauntings at the Inn is the fact that most visitors feel the spirits are profoundly malevolent - the atmosphere has often been described as brooding, oppressive, and even 'evil'. One room, called the Bishop's Room, has the most notorious reputation. One night two men stayed there in the hope of witnessing some ghostly activity - and they had such a terrifying night that they had to summon a vicar to exorcise them.

Over the years, the Inn has been investigated by many paranormal researchers, especially for television shows like Ghost Adventures and Most Haunted. One paranormal expert in particular is Kieron Butler from the UK Paranormal Study. The group, led by Kieron to study in the Ram Inn, consisted of seven people, including photographers and medium/spiritual advisors. The Ghost Club (the oldest paranormal research organization in the world) investigated the inn in 2003, but didn't register anything paranormal. The Danish paranormal research team DPA (Dansk Parapsykologisk Aspekt) has also been there with a TV crew, shooting an episode for a Danish ghost-hunter TV show.

21. Pengersick Castle

Pengersick Castle is a fortified Tudor manor house hidden away in Praa Sands, Cornwall. The oldest part still standing dates from 1500, but there has been a building on this site for at least 900 years. It is reportedly the most haunted castle in Britain.

Many people claim to have encountered some of the 20 odd ghosts said to be here. Many have seen or photographed strange orbs of light. Electrical malfunctions are commonplace. There are massive temperature drops. The ghosts said to be haunting Pengersick Castle include a 14th-century-monk, a 13-year-old girl who danced to her death off the battlements, a 4-year-old boy who tugs at ladies' dresses, the re-enactment of a medieval murder, a woman seen walking through a wall and pacing the room, a woman stabbed to death in the castle, a man stabbed and strangled in 1546 in front of a fireplace, and several previous owners.

The ghost club has carried out many late night vigils at the castle, and there's been a televised display of automatic writing, which resulted in a scribbled picture of a female face.

Pengersick Castle is widely accepted as the most haunted location in the UK, and it has been the subject of many television programmes, as well as getting a mention in numerous books, media and publications. It is a striking building and has many good reasons to make a visit. It's primarily a private residence, but the owners make the house and grounds available as often as they can and are investing in research and digs to find out more about the house and grounds.

The ghost tours continue to be very popular.

22. Tutbury Castle

Situated in the heart of England, Tutbury Castle stands on wooded slopes overlooking the winding River Dove, with spectacular views across the plain of the Dove to the beautiful Derbyshire hills. Occupied since the Stone Age, the castle is first recorded in 1071, as one of the new castles built to stamp the authority of the Norman conquerors across the Midlands. Since then, the castle has played an important part in English history on many occasions, in warfare and in peace. The castle is best known as one of the prisons of Mary Queen of Scots, who was incarcerated there on four occasions. It was here that she became involved in the plot that ultimately led to her bloody execution at Fotheringhay.

Tutbury has a long tradition of ghostly happenings, and here are just a few of the most famous ones:

The Keeper - Wearing a full suit of armour, and behaving in a manner that might best be described as authoritative, this ghostly figure has been seen stepping out in John of Gaunt's Gateway and bellowing "Get thee hence!" Although last sighted in daylight about four years ago, by a visitor who complained that an idiot of an enactor had told him to "get over the fence", recent increases in paranormal activity might suggest that another visit could be imminent. When it was pointed out that no enactors were on site that day, and that similar ghostly apparitions had been reported by other unsuspecting visitors, the response was "I'm sorry, but I don't believe in ghosts".

Mary Queen of Scots - Tutbury was Mary's most despised prison. She suffered much at Tutbury and was at the Castle as a captive of Elizabeth 1st on four occasions. She was seen all in white by some members of Her Majesty's services. In 2004, at approximately midnight, she was seen standing at the top of the South Tower by a group of men - in the form of a figure dressed in a pure white gown. When they saw her, they all just laughed, believing the Curator was just teasing them by putting on an Elizabethan gown as a joke. When it was pointed out that curator Lesley Smith did not have a white gown, and neither did any other Elizabethan enactor working at the Castle, the men were profoundly disturbed by this sighting. She was also seen rapidly crossing the grass, one hot afternoon in 1984, by a serving Marine. Recently, there have been a number of sightings of Mary - especially between 10.15 p.m. and 11.00 p.m. A figure, dressed in black, is seen standing at the window of the Great Hall as cars leave the Castle. In May and June this year, she was not only seen by senior members of staff, who are usually quite dismissive of such reports, but also by archaeologists participating in a seasonal dig at the castle.

Film and TV - Many paranormal TV shows have been recorded at Tutbury Castle. For ghost lovers, the Castle has featured on "Most Haunted" and "The World's Biggest Ghost Hunt." In September 2005, and April 2006, Tutbury Castle hosted the national "Most Haunted" Convention. In October (2004) Tutbury Castle welcomed 2,000 people on a one-night ghost-hunting event! Some visitors come from as far afield as Paris to spend a night in Tutbury.

23. Bodmin Jail

Bodmin Jail is a historic former prison situated in Bodmin, on the edge of Bodmin Moor in Cornwall. Built in 1779 and closed in 1927, the large range of buildings is now largely in ruins, although parts of the prison have been turned into a tourist attraction. The jail was originally built for King George 3rd in 1779 by prisoners of war and was designed by Sir John Call. The jail had enough room to accommodate 100 prisoners. The building which stands today was built in 1860 using 20'000 tonnes of granite from "Cuckoo Quarry" in Bodmin which was fetched by the prisoners. Bodmin was the first jail to feature separate "cells", and each small chamber may well have a nasty story to tell.

During World War 1, the Doomsday Book and the Crown Jewels were kept in Bodmin Jail for safe keeping.

In the 150 years Bodmin jail was operational, it held 50 public executions, the first one being in 1785 and the last in 1909. The executioners were paid around £10 per execution.

In 1927 the jail was closed for good.

With its forbidding aspect and dark history, Bodmin Jail has, not surprisingly, attracted many ghost stories and paranormal researchers over the years - including the crew of the TV show Most Haunted - and there is a ghost walk/night regularly available for tourists.

Matthew Weekes was a prisoner of Bodmin Jail. It was

believed by some that he was wrongly accused of a crime and was imprisoned an innocent man. People visiting the jail claim to have seen Matthew's ghost wandering the cells. A lady named Selina Wadge was executed by hanging at the prison because she murdered her child when it was born out of wedlock. Her spirit is said to haunt the prison, grabbing at visiting children and making pregnant women feel a huge amount of remorse.

Many, many more ghosts have been witnessed at Bodmin prison by people visiting the gloomy and oppressive building.

Today, most of the jail remains in ruins, and presents a forbidding aspect when seen from a distance. Some parts have been refurbished and these now form a tourist attraction with exhibitions telling of the history of the jail and of offenders imprisoned there. The exhibits showcase gory mannequins accompanied with plaques, describing the offence committed by particular persons and their sentence, in their respective cells. Because of the style of exhibit, it has been likened to such attractions as The London Dungeon.

24. Woodchester Mansion

Often said to be one of the most haunted locations in the UK, Woodchester Mansion, built by William Leigh, is a 19th Century Victorian Gothic Masterpiece mysteriously abandoned mid-construction in 1873. Hidden in a secluded Cotswold valley, it is untouched by time and the modern world. This Grade 1 listed building has been saved from dereliction, but will never be completed.

Visitors to the mansion walk through an extraordinary architectural exhibit in which the secrets of the medieval Gothic builders and masons are laid bare. The carvings in Woodchester Mansion are among the finest of their kind in the world.

The ghosts said to haunt Woodchester Mansion evoke tales of the horror the building has seen over the years. Many deaths occurred at the mansion, including workmen and family members, from the previous building that once stood on the foundations. Accidents, murders, and alleged human sacrifices have all added weight to the reputation the mansion has gained for being a hotspot of paranormal activity. On various ghost hunts, the strange phenomena produced at the mansion has stunned and chilled many a seasoned investigator. A cold presence has often been felt with each step taken, dark cloaked figures have been seen wandering the hallways, and voices whispering in the ears of frightened guests are just a few of the regular happenings in the dead of the night. Much of Woodchester's ghostly heritage is reported to be poltergeist in nature.

In 1902, a vicar was reported to have seen a strange apparition at the mansion's gates. A phantom horseman has also been seen on the mansion's drive. It is said that the mansion itself is the epicentre of all the haunting happenings in the area. There is the Tall Man of the Chapel, which has been seen many times, and the elemental in the house's cellar. The mansion is said to be the home of some of the scariest ghosts in the United Kingdom. Visitors have collapsed and have been attacked by the ghostly dwellers of the mansion. There is a floating head, which has been seen by many visitors in one of the bathrooms. There is also the spectre of the old woman who likes to attack female visitors by grabbing them in the dark. It is said that the reason why the mansion is haunted is because it stands on the site of the three previous buildings, which are also haunted.

The mansion has its own chapel, and satanic rituals have been heard in here. People have reported hearing a woman singing an Irish folk song in the scullery. The ghost of a young girl has been seen several times playing and running up and down the stairs of the mansion's first floor.

25. Derby Gaol

Given its colourful history of imprisonment, death, and misery, it's certainly no surprise that Derby Gaol has been dubbed the 'Most haunted Place in Derby'. Over the years, there have been many paranormal occurrences and sightings reported.

According to the owner and staff at the Gaol, the ghostly sightings and incidents tend to occur mostly from around October through to December, and then tail off until June and July when they pick up again.

The Gaol's current owner, Richard Felix - who is also a popular author and TV ghost show presenter - has had several supernatural encounters himself at the Gaol.

For example, one Friday afternoon in November, three years ago, Richard was standing in the kitchen of the Gaol talking on the phone, when a figure walked down the corridor past him. The grey haze was in the form of a person, which glided down the corridor and vanished at the bottom. The experience unnerved him so much that he was unwilling to hang up the phone and brave leaving the Gaol alone. He returned the following year on the anniversary of the sighting at the same time and waited. This time, however, he experienced nothing.

During the revamp and restoration of the Gaol, one of the builders was working in the cells. Twice during the Saturday afternoon, the cell door closed by itself while he was in there. The same builder also had to leave the room several times on account of feeling sick - something he attributed to the coffee he had consumed earlier that day! Many other visitors - including a few TV paranormal show presenters - have also felt nauseous and emotional in the same cell.

Some people find themselves unable to go into the cells, reporting extremely unpleasant feelings. Some that do later leave hurriedly, telling of suffocating feelings, being 'pushed down', and sensations of darkness and sickness. One visitor was so badly affected that she was physically sick.

One gentleman claimed to have witnessed something very disturbing in one of the cells: two dead men hanging from a fixed beam inside the cell. The men were reported as facing the doorway, but turned slightly inwards towards each other, just hanging there. They appeared to have been approximately in their late twenties to early thirties.

The condemned cell has long been an area which has caused discomfort to visitors. Some people have reported 'neck restriction' and feelings of suffocation.

Two ladies, on one occasion, left the Gaol in tears, clutching their throats and feeling unable to breathe. They had felt that 'something' was around their neck.

Exiting the Gaol, they passed a figure standing by the door, which they mistook for an actor. He was bald and wore a sleeveless leather outfit, which the ladies described as looking like a body warmer. This same figure has also been seen in the dayroom, alarming one of the female eyewitnesses who described it as 'evil' and 'a murderer'. This mysterious entity has also been seen by another contractor called Chris, who was also working on the restoration of the Gaol. He saw the figure while locking up alone one night.

True Ghost Stories

He also described the bald figure as wearing 'fancy dress' - a leather 'body warmer'. The figure walked away, passing through a cigarette machine, and disappeared through the wall.

A lady in a large 'Ascot' type hat has also been seen at a time when the Gaol was a drinking venue known as 'The Secret Place'. The figure walked down the corridor, through a door, and presumably up the steps beyond. The three men who had witnessed it followed her. They opened the door and ascended the steps outside to the top, only to find a heavy carpet of snow. There were no footprints to be found anywhere.

One lady decided to spend the night alone in the condemned man's cell. Initially, nothing happened, until the early hours, when she began to hear noises and footsteps. Something tugged her sleeping bag off, and as she tried to grab it, she dropped her pillow. When she turned back, her pillow had vanished. She had to turn on her flashlight in order to try and find it, only to discover it near the cell door, almost 10ft away from where she had dropped it.

After one of the Derby Ghostwalks several years ago, everyone was sitting in the dayroom finishing their dinner while their guide, Peter, finished his summing up for the evening. One of the diners noticed a figure suspended from the wood above the doorway, swinging gently behind the guide. Initially, the man presumed that it was an actor, or one of the 'scares' from the tour. He soon realised this was not so when no one else noticed the hanging figure.

There have been incidents of poltergeist activity in the Gaol. Cups and saucers moving or flying through the air of their own accord. Richard Felix, the current owner, had a pair of original 18th century spectacles vanish, which turned

Alan Toner

up three months later by the main door in a very prominent place.

About The Author

Alan Toner was born on Merseyside. He has always enjoyed writing, and has had many of his articles and short stories published in various magazines and books.

In addition to his True Ghost Stories books, he has also published two volumes of his Horror Stories series on Amazon. In between his writing, he also runs the True Ghost Stories website at www.trueghoststories.co.uk

Official website: www.wirralwriter.co.uk

Facebook Page: https://www.facebook.com/mersey.male1

Twitter Profile: Scouselad8

If you enjoyed this book, Alan would really appreciate it if you could leave a review for it on Amazon.

Printed in Great Britain
by Amazon